Horizons

Preschool
For Three's

BIBLE STORY
READER

Author/Editor:	Rachelle Wiersma, M.A.
Managing Editor:	Alan Christopherson, M.S.
Copy Editors:	Pamela Ufen
	Anita Lanning
Designer & Illustrator:	Anthony Kuhlmann

Alpha Omega Publications • Rock Rapids, Iowa

©MMXIII by Alpha Omega Publications, a division of Glynlyon Inc.®

804 N. 2nd Ave. E., Rock Rapids, IA 51246-1759

All rights reserved.

Scripture quotations marked (NIV) are taken from the Holy Bible, New International Version®, NIV®. Copyright © 1973, 1978, 1984, 2011 by Biblica, Inc.™ Used by permission of Zondervan. All rights reserved worldwide. www.zondervan.com The "NIV" and "New International Version" are trademarks registered in the United States Patent and Trademark Office by Biblica, Inc.™

Printed in the United States of America

ISBN 978-0-7403-2998-2

PREFACE

The Bible Story Reader is composed of 40 Bible stories. The selections include 20 Old Testament and 20 New Testament selections. Each selection includes a simple retelling of the Bible story suitable for a three-year-old. However, if you have older children, they may enjoy the reading as well. A work of art depicts each selection. These rich illustrations bring the story to life for the young student. Included with the story and picture are a number of thought questions to help you further engage the student in the story. At times these questions can extend the lessons learned into the student's life. Each Bible story concludes with a simple prayer. The student workbook includes at least one activity for each Bible story.

A new Bible story is also presented each week. You may want to read and discuss the Bible story each day you have class. Students at this age enjoy having stories read and reread to them. Eventually the student may want to look at the picture and tell you the story.

CONTENTS

CONTENTS

Creation

Long before you were born or your parents or grandparents were born, God created the world and everything in it. God spoke and there was grass. God spoke again and there were birds flying in the air. God created all the trees, mountains, and animals in the world. God also created two special people. He named the man Adam. He named the woman Eve. He created a beautiful world for them. God also made this world for you to enjoy.

_____

Thought Questions:
Look at the picture of how an artist viewed God's creation. What types of plants do you see? What are some of the animals in the picture? If you were to draw a picture of God's creation, what animals would you include? One of the jobs God gave Adam was to name the animals. Adam looked at each animal and gave it a name. He saw an animal with a long neck and called it a giraffe. He saw a friendly animal that wagged its tail and called it a dog. God gave Adam his name. What name did your parents give you? Your name is very special.

Prayer:
Dear Jesus, Thank You for making the world. Thank You for making animals like dogs, cats, and dolphins. Thank You for making people to live in Your world. Amen.

Sin

Adam and Eve lived in the Garden of Eden. They could eat from every tree in the garden except one. Satan told them that the fruit from that tree was the best. Adam and Eve wanted to taste the fruit. When they took a bite, they sinned against God. Adam and Eve could no longer live in the garden. They would have to work hard to find food. Weeds would grow that needed to be pulled. They were sad they had not listened to God.

_____

Thought Questions:
Do you remember the picture of the garden from the first Bible story you read? What beautiful things did you see in that picture? Look at the picture of this Bible story. Adam and Eve are the people in the picture. Notice how sad they look. Why do you think they are sad? The angel is sending them from the perfect Garden of Eden. They will not be able to return. Instead, they will have to work hard to make things grow. Do you ever do things that are wrong? When we sin, we pray to God that He will forgive us. We also pray that He will help keep us from doing those bad things again.

Prayer:
Dear Jesus, I am sorry when I sin and do things that are wrong. Thank You for forgiving me of those sins. Help me not to do things that are wrong and hurt others. Amen.

Noah

A long time ago God told Noah He was going to send a flood. The flood would cover all the trees, hills, and mountains. Noah needed to build a big boat. The boat was called an ark. Noah was to put two of every kind of animal in the ark. He and his family would live in the ark and take care of the animals. Noah, his family, and the animals would be kept safe during the flood. After the flood, God sent a rainbow. The rainbow reminded Noah and his family that God would never again send a flood that would cover the entire earth.

_____

Thought Questions:

Point to the large ark in the middle of the picture. Name some of the animals you see walking into the ark. You can see that there are two of the animals. There are two horses at the front of the picture. Do you see the dark clouds in the picture? Soon it will begin to rain. All the animals need to get into the ark so Noah can take care of them. Is there an animal you would like to care for? What would you need to do to take care of that animal? Why did God send a rainbow?

Prayer:

Dear Jesus, Thank You for saving Noah, his family, and the animals from the flood. Thank You for sending the rainbow. Thank You for taking care of my family and me. Amen.

Tower of Babel

One day some people started building a tower that would reach high into the sky. They thought if they built this tower they would be powerful like God. God saw what they were doing. He was unhappy with their plans. God confused the languages of the people building the tower. This meant that the builders no longer understood each other. Soon work on the tower stopped. The people learned that they were not more powerful than God.

_____

Thought Questions:
Do you see the big tower in the picture? Do you see how it goes into the clouds? Notice the people building the tower. See how small they look? Have you ever seen a really tall building? Many cities have tall buildings. Building a tall building is not wrong. What is wrong is thinking that you can be as powerful as God. God created the mighty mountains. God also created the smallest flowers. God has created things that no person can.

Prayer:
Dear Jesus. Thank You for being a powerful God who loves me. Thank You for the many things You have made. Thank You for creating big things like tall trees and little things like ladybugs. Amen.

Moses

Many years ago God's people, called the Israelites, lived in the land of Egypt. The leader of Egypt was called Pharaoh. Pharaoh did not like God's people. He made a law that the Israelites could not keep their baby boys. One family tried to save their baby boy. They knew that Pharaoh's daughter went to the Nile River to bathe. The family put their baby boy in a basket in the river. Pharaoh's daughter saw the baby and immediately loved him. She decided to save the baby and raise him as her son. This baby was named Moses. God would use Moses to lead the Israelites out of Egypt.

_____

Thought Questions:
Point to the baby in the picture. Point to Pharaoh's daughter. Do you remember why the baby is in a basket? The princess is leaning over to look at the baby. What did the princess name the baby? She loved the baby and wanted to care for him. How do your parents take care of you? God loved the baby Moses. God also loves you.

Prayer:
Dear Jesus, Thank You for protecting baby Moses. Thank You for giving him a loving family. Thank You for my family who loves me and takes care of me. Amen.

Burning Bush

As Moses grew, he saw how the Egyptians used God's people as slaves. This made him sad and angry. When Moses saw an Egyptian hurt an Israelite, he hurt the Egyptian. Because of this, he had to leave Egypt. He went to live in the desert where he cared for sheep. One day as he was working, he saw a bush that was burning. As he looked closer, he saw that the bush did not burn up. When Moses came toward the bush, he heard a voice. God was speaking to Moses. God told Moses that He had an important job for him. Moses was to lead God's people out of Egypt. The Israelites would no longer be slaves.

Thought Questions:
Why did Moses have to leave Egypt? What work did Moses do in the desert? What unusual thing did Moses see? Do you see the burning bush in the picture? When Moses came close to the bush what did he hear? What work did God have for him? God has work for you and your family too. Ask your parents what work God has for them. What kind of work does God have for you?

Prayer:
Dear Jesus, Thank You for speaking to Moses and giving him a special job. Thank You for the work You have given to my family. Thank You for the work You have given to me. Help me to do my best in all my work. Amen.

Plagues

Moses did what God said and went back to Egypt. He spoke to the ruler of Egypt who was called Pharaoh. Moses told Pharaoh to let God's people go. Pharaoh refused. He did not want to lose his slaves. Moses told Pharaoh that if he didn't listen, God would send plagues to Egypt. A plague is a very big problem that would hurt many people. The first plague God sent to Egypt made the river water bad. This meant the people could not drink the water and the fish would die. When Pharaoh still wouldn't let the people go, God sent other plagues. These included large numbers of frogs, flies, locust, and hailstorms. God sent a total of ten plagues to Egypt. After the last plague, Pharaoh finally agreed to let the Israelites leave Egypt.

Thought Questions:

Can you say the word "plague?" What is a plague? Why did God send plagues to Egypt? Do you remember any of the plagues God sent? One of the plagues God sent was frogs. What do you think it would be like to have a house full of frogs? Are there places you would not like to find a frog? One way we can listen to God is by reading the Bible. The Bible storybook you are holding is one way to learn more about God.

Prayer:

Dear Jesus, Thank You for the Bible. Thank You for teaching me through the Bible stories I'm learning. Help me to listen carefully to these stories. Help me to obey You. Amen.

Red Sea

Moses and the Israelites had just left Egypt when Pharaoh changed his mind. He wanted to keep the Israelites as slaves. Pharaoh and his army chased the Israelites. Soon Moses and the people reached the Red Sea. They had no way to get across. They could see Pharaoh's army behind them. The Israelites were worried they would have to go back to a life of slavery. God told Moses to take his staff and stretch it out over the sea. God made a dry path through the water. The Israelites could now cross the Red Sea on dry ground. Once all the Israelites were safely on the other side, the water returned to cover the path. The Egyptians could not follow the Israelites. God saved His people from the Egyptians.

Thought Questions:
Do you see the tall man with the white hair in the picture? That is Moses. What does he have in his hand? What is he doing with his staff? Look at the water. Notice how it has been parted to create a path. The Israelites will walk across the path to the other side. Do you remember what happened after they reached the other side? Once they knew they were safe, Moses and his sister Miriam led the Israelites in song. The people danced as they sang, "Sing to the LORD, for he is highly exalted. The horse and its rider he has hurled into the sea." Exodus 15:21 (NIV).

Prayer:
Dear Jesus, Thank You for saving the Israelites. Thank You for showing Your power by parting the Red Sea. Thank You for the song that Miriam and Moses sang to You. Bless me as I sing songs to You too. Amen.

Food in the Desert

The people of Israel lived in the desert for 40 years. A desert is a dry place. Few plants grow in a desert. There were many Israelites who needed to be fed. No grocery stores could be found in the desert either. God sent His people a very special food called manna. The people gathered the manna and cooked it in a variety of ways. Each day manna would fall and the people would gather it. As long as they lived in the desert, God provided manna. When they reached the land of Canaan, God no longer sent manna.

_____

Thought Questions:

Look at the people in the picture. They are filling baskets with manna. God sent enough manna for each day. On the last day of the week, they were to gather twice as much manna. This way the people would not work the next day. That day was set apart to worship God. How do you make Sunday a special day to worship God? Do you go to church? Do you spend time with the family God gave you? Maybe you can think of a special way you can worship God on Sunday.

Prayer:

Dear Jesus, Thank You for providing me with food each day. Thank You for the people that make the food for me. Thank You for Sunday, a special day to worship You. Help me find ways to serve You on Sunday. Amen.

A New Home

God's people finally arrived at their new home. God had promised that one day they would live in Canaan. The people were excited to see this Promised Land. There were wonderful fruits and vegetables growing in the land. No longer would they live in the desert. However, there were other people living in the land. These people did not love or worship God. The Israelites would have to fight in order to take the land. God would be with His people as they fought their enemies.

Thought Questions:

Moving to a new home can be an exciting and scary experience. Have you ever moved to a new home? Have you ever moved to a different bedroom in your home? What things do you think you would miss if you moved to a new home? The Israelites were worried about moving to a new home. They would have to get used to different types of food. They would have different neighbors. They were also excited. This was the home God had promised them. They would no longer have to live in tents.

Prayer:

Dear Jesus, Thank You for bringing the Israelites to their new home. Thank You for caring for them in the desert. Thank You for giving me a home. Help me to take care of the home You have given me. Amen.

Jericho

Other people lived in the land God promised His people. These people had built cities and homes. They did not love or follow God like the Israelites. God wanted His people to live in and care for the land of Canaan. After Moses died, God chose Joshua as Israel's leader. Joshua would lead the Israelites in conquering Canaan. In order to enter Canaan, the Israelites needed to capture the city of Jericho. The city had tall walls and a large army. God had an unusual way for the Israelites to take the city. He ordered the Israelites to march around the city once for six days. On the seventh day, they were to march around the city seven times with the priests blowing trumpets. After the final trumpet blast, the people were to shout and the walls would come down. When this happened, the people knew that God had given them the city. He was on their side.

Thought Questions:

Can you say the names Joshua and Jericho? Do you remember the special plan God had for conquering Jericho? How many days were the Israelites to march once around the city? How many times were they to march around the city the last day? When were the people to shout so that the walls came down? Do you think you could shout and bring down a wall? Do you think if your entire family shouted together they could bring down a wall? We know that only God could use the shouts of the people to bring down the thick, tall walls of Jericho.

Prayer:

Dear Jesus, Thank You for being a mighty God. We know that You can do powerful things. Help me to follow You every day. Forgive me when I do wrong. Amen.

Hannah's Prayer

A woman named Hannah lived in Israel. More than anything else she wanted a baby. She prayed to God every day that He would give her a child. Once a year she went with her husband to Shiloh. A special place was built there for the people to worship God. Each year she said the same prayer. She asked God for a child. One year a priest named Eli saw her praying. She told Eli her desire to have a child. Eli told her that God would give her what she asked. When the baby was born, she named her baby Samuel. When Samuel was old enough, he would go and live with the priest Eli. Samuel would help Eli in serving God.

_____

Thought Questions:

Is there anything you have ever wanted? Some people pray to God for things they want or need. Sometimes God's answer is yes. He agrees that this is something they should have. Sometimes God's answer is no. He doesn't think that they need the thing. Other times, God's answer is to wait. God knows what is best for His people. He knows if what you pray for is something you should have, should not have, or should wait to have. It is important to trust that God knows what is best for you, because you are His special child.

Prayer:

Dear Jesus, Thank You for knowing what's best for me. Help me to accept Your answers of yes, no, and wait. Thank You for listening to my prayers. Amen.

God Speaks to Samuel

One night when Samuel was almost asleep, he heard a voice calling to him. Samuel thought it was Eli. He went to Eli's bedroom to see if the priest needed him. Eli told Samuel that he had not called him. This happened three times. After the third time, Eli told Samuel that God was calling him. Samuel was to say to God, "Speak, for Your servant is listening." The next time God called, Samuel answered as Eli had told him. Samuel listened to what God had to say. Samuel would serve as a leader for the people of Israel. It was important that Samuel learned to listen to God.

_____

Thought Questions:

Can you point to Samuel and Eli in the picture? Who did Samuel think was calling him? Who did Eli say was calling him? What did God tell Samuel? Why was it important that Samuel listened to God? God has given you parents who call you. It is important that you listen to what they say. Sometimes your parents call to you to keep you from danger. Parents can also call because they need to see you or have something for you. No matter when they call, it is important to answer the parents God gave you.

Prayer:

Dear Jesus, Thank You for the parents You have given me. Help me to listen and answer when they call me. Forgive me when I do not listen. Amen.

David and Goliath

Even though they had conquered Canaan, the Israelites still found themselves at war. The Philistines were a neighboring nation that often went to war with Israel. One of their soldiers was a giant named Goliath. Every day he came out from his camp and made fun of God and the Israelites. A boy named David came to the Israelite camp to visit his brothers who were soldiers. When he heard Goliath mock God and the Israelites, he decided he needed to stop him. Armed with his slingshot, David planned to defeat Goliath. David knew that God was on his side. He stopped by a stream and chose five smooth stones. He put one of the stones in his slingshot, aimed, and threw it. The stone struck Goliath in the head. With God's help, David had saved the Israelites from Goliath and the Philistines.

Thought Questions:

Can you say the names Goliath and David? Who was taller and stronger—David or Goliath? Who do you think the Philistines and Israelites thought would win a battle between David and Goliath? Who did win? Why do you think David was able to beat Goliath? David trusted in God. He knew he could not beat Goliath unless God was on his side. David loved God, and God loved David. One day David would rule as the King of Israel.

Prayer:

Dear Jesus, Thank You for being with David when he defeated Goliath. Thank You for being with me every day. Help me to always follow You. Amen.

David and Jonathan

After David killed Goliath, he became famous in Israel. Everyone knew who he was. The king of Israel, Saul, was jealous. He wanted people to pay more attention to him. One of King Saul's sons was named Jonathan. Jonathan became good friends with David. Jonathan knew that God loved David. Jonathan loved David and God. Jonathan warned David when the king was angry. Sometimes King Saul tried to hurt David. Jonathan made sure that David was safe. Jonathan knew that God had a special plan for David, who would one day be the king of Israel.

Thought Questions:
God gives people the gift of friends. Friends can be neighbors, cousins, and people from church. Some friends you might see every day and others not as often. What things do you like to do with a friend? How can you be a good friend? Jonathan and David were good friends. They both loved God. It is important that you find friends who love God too.

Prayer:
Dear Jesus, Thank You for giving me friends. Help me to find friends who love You. Please help me be a good friend to others. Amen.

Psalm 150

David Writes Psalms

Throughout his life David wrote poems and songs to praise God. These poems and songs were called Psalms. One entire book of the Bible contains David's Psalms to God. In some of the Psalms, David told God about his problems. In others he asked God to save him from his enemies. David also praised God and sang joyfully to Him. There are 150 Psalms in the Bible. The very last psalm told of the ways in which God could be praised. David wrote, "Praise him with tambourine and dancing, praise him with the strings and flute, praise him with the clash of cymbals." Psalm 150:4–5 (NIV). By writing psalms, David was able to tell how he felt to God.

_____

Thought Questions:
When you go to church you probably hear people singing. They are praising God with their voices. Some of the words that they sing come from David's book of Psalms. Even though these were written many years ago, they are still used to praise God. Have you learned any songs of praise to God? Practice the songs that you have learned to give praise to God.

Prayer:
Dear Jesus, like David, I want to praise You. I thank You for the beautiful world You created. Thank You for words and music that help me give praise to You. Amen.

Esther Becomes Queen

The people of Israel sinned against God and were conquered by the Persians. The Persians were ruled by a king named Xerxes. The king became unhappy with his queen and he wanted a new one. He decided to hold a beauty pageant. Among the young women chosen for the pageant was an Israelite named Esther. Her uncle, Mordecai, had raised her. He taught her to love God. When the time came for Esther to meet King Xerxes, he wanted her as his queen. She was not only beautiful, but she was also kind. Esther married King Xerxes and became his new queen.

_____

Thought Questions:
Can you say the names Xerxes, Mordecai, and Esther? Who was Mordecai? He raised Esther to love God, just as your parents are doing. Who was Xerxes? Some kings do not follow God and so they sin against God. King Xerxes sinned by wanting a new queen. Who was Esther? God blessed Esther for loving Him and being a kind person.

Prayer:
Dear Jesus, Thank You for giving me parents who teach me about You. Thank You for the story of Esther found in the Bible. Help me to be like Esther in loving You and being kind. Amen.

Esther Saves Her People

Do you remember the last story about Queen Esther? She was married to King Xerxes of Persia. The king did not know that Esther was an Israelite. One of the king's advisors hated the Israelites. His name was Haman, and he planned to hurt all of God's people. Esther's uncle heard of the plan. He told her she had to go to the king and ask him to help her people. Esther was scared. She did not know if the king would talk to her. Her uncle told her that he and all the Israelites would pray for her. When Esther appeared before Xerxes, he was glad to see her. She explained Haman's plan to hurt the Israelites. The king was very angry with Haman and had him punished. He made sure the Israelites would not be hurt as Haman had planned. God used Esther to save His people.

_____

Thought Questions:

Haman hated the people of Israel. He wanted to hurt them. Did he know that Esther was an Israelite? Did King Xerxes know that Esther was an Israelite? At the time Esther lived, she could not see her husband, the king, unless he asked to see her. If she went to him without permission, he could order her to be punished. This was why the people of Israel prayed for her. What happened when Esther approached the king? God heard the prayers of His people and saved them. God hears your prayers as well.

Prayer:

Dear Jesus, Thank You for hearing our prayers. Thank You for listening to me when I am happy or have a problem. Amen.

Jonah and the Big Fish

Jonah was a prophet of God. That means he told people about God. When people disobeyed God, it was Jonah's job to tell them they had sinned. Then the people would stop sinning and obey God. Most of the time Jonah spoke to the people of Israel, but one day God told Jonah to tell the people of Nineveh to stop sinning. Nineveh was a city in the country of Israel's enemy, Assyria. Jonah did not want to go to Nineveh. He did not want the people to stop sinning and be forgiven. Jonah wanted God to punish them. Jonah decided he wasn't going to listen to God. He got on a ship to go to a city far away. While they were sailing, a sudden storm came up on the ocean. The sailors were afraid. Jonah knew God sent the storm because he hadn't gone to Nineveh. Jonah told the sailors to throw him over the side of the ship. If they did, the storm would stop and the sailors would be safe. They did what Jonah asked and they were saved. God sent a great fish to swallow Jonah. He would be safe inside the fish for three days before the fish spit him out on land.

Thought Questions:

Can you say the word "Nineveh?" What kind of city was Nineveh? Nineveh was a wicked city. They did sinful things. Still, God wanted them to stop sinning and obey Him. Do you remember the name of the person God wanted to go to Nineveh? Why didn't Jonah want to go? Jonah thought he could run away from God. You know that God sees everything we do. What happened to the ship Jonah was on? How did Jonah say the storm would stop? God sent a giant fish to save Jonah. Do you remember how many days Jonah had to stay inside the big fish?

Prayer:

Dear Jesus, Forgive me when I sin and do wrong. Help me to obey You and listen to Your Word. Thank You for loving me even when I sin. Amen.

Jonah Preaches in Nineveh

After Jonah had been in the fish for three days, he was spit out on shore. Once again God told Jonah to preach to the people of Nineveh. This time Jonah obeyed. He told the people that if they didn't obey, God would destroy the city. The people of Nineveh believed Jonah's message from God. They turned from their sinful ways. They fasted, which meant they didn't eat, and they wore sackcloth instead of nice clothes. They wanted God to see how sorry they were for sinning. Even the king took off his royal clothing and put on sackcloth. He told all the people to stop sinning and pray to God. God saw how the people of Nineveh had stopped sinning and were sorry. God did not destroy the city.

Thought Questions:

When we do something that hurts someone, it is important that we say we're sorry. The people of Nineveh knew they had hurt God by sinning. How did they show they were sorry? One way people in Jonah's time showed they were sorry was by fasting. This meant for a day or more they wouldn't eat. Another way they would show they were sorry was by wearing sackcloth. This was a rough material that people used to store grain or vegetables. The rough material reminded the people of their sins. What are some ways that you show God and others that you are sorry for what you said or did? One thing you should always do is pray to God for forgiveness.

Prayer:

Dear Jesus, Thank You for saving Jonah and the people of Nineveh. Help me not to sin and do bad things. Please forgive me when I sin. Amen.

Jesus' Birth

God sent an angel to a young woman named Mary. The angel told her she would be the mother of God's son, Jesus. Mary and her husband Joseph needed to travel to Bethlehem. When they reached the town, all the rooms for the travelers were filled. They asked the innkeeper if there was any place they could stay. He said they could stay in his stable, which was a place where animals lived. Jesus was born in a stable. Mary placed Him in a manger because there was no crib.

Thought Questions:

At Christmas time we celebrate the birth of Jesus. What special things happen at your church or home to celebrate the birth of Jesus? One of the songs many children sing at Christmas is, "Away In a Manger"

> Away in a manger, no crib for a bed,
> The little Lord Jesus laid down His sweet head.
> The stars in the sky looked down where He lay,
> The little Lord Jesus, asleep on the hay.

The song reminds us that Jesus was born in a stable and placed in a manger. Sing this song together, and if you know the actions, do those as well.

Prayer:

Dear Jesus, Thank You for coming to earth as a baby. Thank You for Mary and Joseph who took care of You. Thank You for giving me a family to care for me. Amen.

The Shepherds Visit Jesus

On the night Jesus was born, there were shepherds in the field near Bethlehem. They were watching their sheep and keeping them from danger. Suddenly the night sky was filled with angels. The shepherds were afraid. They had never seen a sky filled with angels. The angels said, "Glory to God." An angel told the shepherds of the birth of God's son, Jesus. When the angels left, the shepherds hurried to Bethlehem to see Jesus. They reached the stable and saw the baby. They told everyone they knew about what they had heard and seen.

Thought Questions:
Have you ever been outside on a dark night? Imagine that suddenly that dark sky was filled with angels. You might be afraid or surprised at such as scene. The shepherds were afraid when they saw all the angels. The angel's first words to the shepherds were, "Do not be afraid." The angels had something important they wanted to tell the shepherds. Do you remember what news the angels had for the shepherds? They told them that Jesus was born in Bethlehem. That is good news that we must also tell others.

Prayer:
Dear Jesus, Thank You for sending angels to tell the shepherds of Your birth. Help me to worship You like the shepherds did. Like the shepherds, help me tell others about You. Amen.

The Wise Men

At the time of Jesus' birth, some wise men were studying the stars. They noticed an unusual star moving across the sky. The wise men decided to follow the star to see where it led. They traveled many miles before the star finally stopped above a house. Jesus was no longer living in the stable by the time the wise men came. When they arrived, the wise men were happy to see Jesus. The wise men bowed down and worshiped God's son, Jesus. They gave Him gifts of gold, frankincense, and myrrh. Later, the men returned to their home country.

Thought Questions:

When you were born, your parents made phone calls, sent emails, or wrote letters to tell people about your birth. People were told your name, the date you were born, and even how much you weighed. Your grandparents were excited to hold you and see pictures of you. Other people came to your home with presents. They wanted to celebrate your birth with your family. Jesus' birth was also celebrated. Whom did God send to tell the shepherds of Jesus' birth? How did the wise men learn that Jesus was born? What presents did they bring? God used very special ways to tell people about the birth of His Son, Jesus.

Prayer:

Dear Jesus, Thank You for sending a special star to tell of Your birth. Thank You for the wise men that came to bow down and worship You. Help me to worship You as well. Amen.

Jesus Calls the Disciples

Jesus preached to many people during His life. He asked a group of twelve men to be His disciples or special followers. The men would help Him as He traveled from town to town. They would be able to tell people Jesus' message after He returned to heaven. Some of the men Jesus called were fishermen. They were on their boats fishing when Jesus called them to follow Him. The fishermen left their boats and nets on the shore to be with Jesus. The rest of the men had other jobs. Each one stopped what he was doing to follow Jesus. The names of these men were Simon, whom He also named Peter, Andrew, James, John, Philip, Bartholomew, Matthew who was also called Levi, Thomas, James the son of Alphaeus, Simon the Zealot, Judas the son of James, and Judas Iscariot.

Thought Questions:

Look at the picture in the lesson. Do you see the men on the boat? The men on the boat were fishing. When Jesus lived, people did not have boats with motors. They used boats with sails and oars to go out onto the lake. They would put large nets in the water next to the boat. They would catch fish in these nets. Do you see Jesus on the shore? What did he ask the fishermen to do? Jesus told the fishermen that they would no longer catch fish. Instead they would become fishers of men. This meant that they would tell people how to follow Christ. Jesus asks people today to follow Him as well. People are to tell others about Christ so they can follow Him too.

Prayer:

Dear Jesus, Thank You for coming to earth to preach to the people. I am glad that the disciples followed You. Help me to follow You and tell others about You. Amen

Lame Man Through the Roof

Each day that Jesus preached, people crowded around Him. They wanted to hear everything Jesus said. Jesus also healed the sick. People brought their sick family members and friends to Jesus. One day, people crowded into a home where He was preaching. Four friends came to the home with their friend who could not walk. As they came to the house, the friends realized they could not get inside. Homes in this town had flat roofs. The friends decided to climb to the top of the roof with their friend. They took out part of the ceiling so they could lower their friend to Jesus. They put the man who was paralyzed on a mat and gently let him down through the opening. Jesus saw the man and his caring friends. He told the man to stand up, carry his mat, and go home. The man became well and did exactly what Jesus said. The people in the room praised God for the miracle Jesus performed.

Thought Questions:

Do you see the hole in the roof? Why were the people on the roof lowering a man down to the floor? Why did they want him to see Jesus? What happened when the man who was paralyzed met Jesus? The man in this story had very good friends. They were willing to carry him to Jesus. The four friends wanted to do what was best for the man. Imagine the joy of the man after Jesus healed him. The friends were happy as well. Their friend could run, jump, and walk with them again. Friends can help each other when they are hurt. Friends can also celebrate together when good things happen.

Prayer:

Dear Jesus, Thank You for the gift of friends. Thank You for friends who care about me when I am hurt. Thank You for friends who are happy when I am. Help me to be a good friend like the four men in the story. Amen.

Woman at the Well

People who lived in the country where Jesus lived did not like people from Samaria. They treated people from Samaria unkindly. One day Jesus needed to travel through Samaria. Tired and thirsty, Jesus sat down next to a well. When a Samaritan woman came to the well, He asked her for a drink of water. The woman was surprised that someone like Jesus would even talk to her. She gave Jesus water and He treated her with kindness. Jesus told her about God. She learned that Jesus was the Son of God and she believed in Him.

_____

Thought Questions:
Have you ever had people treat you unkindly? Have you ever been unkind to someone? In today's Bible story, there was a Samaritan woman whom people had treated unkindly. How did Jesus treat her? What did the woman learn when Jesus talked to her? What can you learn from Jesus' actions? There are many ways you can show kindness to other people. Some of these include sharing your toys, picking up your things, and saying please and thank you. Think of some ways that you can show kindness to someone today.

Prayer:
Dear Jesus, Thank You for showing me how to be kind to others. Help me to be kind to all people. Forgive me when I am not kind to others. Amen.

Jesus Calms the Storm

One day Jesus asked His disciples to sail with Him across the Sea of Galilee. Many of Jesus' disciples were very good sailors. Jesus was tired and soon fell asleep in the boat. While He was sleeping, a sudden storm came. The wind blew strong, and the waves splashed over the boat. The disciples were afraid and did not know what to do. They woke up Jesus. Seeing their fear, Jesus told the wind and waves to be calm. The disciples were amazed at how the wind and the waves obeyed Jesus. They were no longer afraid.

Thought Questions:

Have you ever been afraid in a storm? What do you do when you are afraid? Many children call to their parents when they are scared. Others may crawl under the blankets in their beds so they do not hear the thunder. In the Bible story, Jesus' disciples were afraid of a storm. What did the disciples do? They woke Jesus. He calmed the storm and they were no longer afraid. When you are afraid, you can pray to Jesus to calm your fears.

Prayer:

Dear Jesus, Thank You for always being near me. When I am afraid, please calm my fears. Help me to remember that You care for me and my family. Amen.

Raising of Jairus' Daughter

As Jesus traveled from town to town, crowds came to welcome Him. At one town a man named Jairus came and fell at Jesus' feet. His young daughter was dying. He wanted Jesus to come to his house to heal her. Before Jesus could leave, news reached Jairus that his daughter had died. Jesus told Jairus not to be afraid. He would go to Jairus' house and heal the girl. When Jesus arrived, the people in the house were weeping. Jesus took the girl's mother, father, and three of His disciples into her room. Jesus told the child to get up. She awoke and got up. Jesus brought the little girl back to life. Everyone was very happy.

Thought Questions:
Jairus was an important man in his town. He helped many people with their problems. But he could not help his sick daughter. Jairus went to Jesus to ask for help. What sad news did he receive while he was with Jesus? He received news that his daughter had died. What happened when Jesus went to the girl's room? Jesus brought her back to life. Jesus showed His love for Jairus' family by bringing the little girl back to life.

Prayer:
Dear Jesus, Thank You for raising Jairus' daughter from the dead. Thank You for caring for little children like me. Help me to show that I care for others too. Amen.

Jesus Feeds 5,000

Great crowds would walk for many miles to hear Jesus speak. Jesus saw that the people were getting hungry. Jesus asked the disciples what food there was to feed the crowd. The disciples said there was very little food and they didn't have enough money to buy any more. One disciple found a boy with five small loaves of bread and two fish. The disciples knew there was not enough food for the 5,000 people in the crowd. Jesus told the disciples to have all the people sit down. He gave thanks and told the people to eat as much as they wanted. Much to the crowd's surprise, there was enough food for everyone. In fact, the disciples collected twelve baskets of leftovers. Jesus used five loaves and two fish to feed 5,000 people and He still had leftovers.

Thought Questions:
Do you see all the people in the picture? They came to hear Jesus. In their excitement, most of them forgot to pack food to eat. Do you see the boy in the picture? He was willing to share his food with others. But how could five loaves and two fish feed all those people? What miracle did Jesus perform? Was there enough food for everyone? There was more than enough food! The disciples collected twelve baskets of leftovers.

Prayer:
Dear Jesus, Bless the food I eat today. Help it to strengthen my body. Thank You for the people who prepare the food for me. Amen.

Jesus Walks on the Water

Jesus' disciples were in a boat crossing the Sea of Galilee. The night was dark and Jesus was not with them. When they reached the middle of the lake it began to storm. The wind blew and the waves were very big. As they looked over the water, they saw a man coming toward them. He was not in a boat. He was walking on the stormy water. The disciples were scared. Jesus was the person walking on the water. He called to them, "It is I; don't be afraid," Matt. 14:27 (NIV). Once Jesus came near, they helped Him into the boat. The seas calmed and they safely reached the shore.

Thought Questions:
Do you see the picture of the men in the boat? Was Jesus in the boat with the disciples? Where was He? Jesus was walking on the water. Can you walk on water? Can your mom or dad walk on water? By walking on water Jesus performed another miracle for the disciples. This showed the disciples that Jesus was God's Son.

Prayer:
Dear Jesus, Thank You for being our great God. You are all-powerful and can walk on water. Help me to trust in You and not be afraid. Amen.

Lazarus

Two sisters and a brother, named Mary, Martha, and Lazarus, were good friends of Jesus. Jesus often stayed with their family as He traveled. When Lazarus became ill, his sisters sent for Jesus. They wanted Jesus to heal their brother. When Jesus arrived, He found Lazarus was dead and placed in a tomb. Jesus saw that Mary and Martha were crying, and He began to weep as well. Jesus asked to be taken to Lazarus' tomb, which was like a cave. He told the men to move the stone from the entrance. Jesus prayed to God and called for Lazarus to come out. Much to the people's amazement, Lazarus walked out of the tomb. Jesus had raised His friend Lazarus from the dead. The sad tears of the people were turned to joyful ones.

Thought Questions:
During Jesus' ministry He traveled from town to town. Sometimes He would stay with His disciples' families. Other times He stayed with friends. Today's story was about three of those friends. Do you remember their names? What happened to Mary and Martha's brother Lazarus? When a person dies, many people come to comfort the family. This was true when Lazarus died. The sisters were eager to see Jesus and have Him share their sadness. While Jesus shared their sorrow, He knew they would soon be happy again. What did Jesus do that brought them joy?

Prayer:
Dear Jesus, I know that You can do all things. Thank You for raising Your friend Lazarus from the dead. Thank You for being my friend. Amen.

Jesus and the Lepers

Many people came to Jesus wanting to be healed from their diseases. One of these diseases was leprosy. People with leprosy could not live near others. The disease could easily pass from one person to another. Ten lepers heard Jesus was coming to a nearby village. From far away they called out to Jesus. They asked Jesus to heal them. Jesus healed all ten of the men. They would now be able to go home to their friends and family. Sadly, only one returned to thank Jesus. The one man knew that Jesus had given him a very special gift. He would no longer need to live far away from other people.

Thought Questions:

Please and thank you are two important things to know how to say. When you need something or want help, you say please. What did the ten lepers in the story ask Jesus to do? They wanted Jesus to heal them from their disease. You also know that it is important to say "thank you" after someone has given you something or helps you. What did the ten men do after Jesus healed them? Only one returned to talk to Jesus. What did he do that was different than the others? Think of people who help you during the day. Make sure to say thank you for the help they give you.

Prayer:

Dear Jesus, Please be with me today in all that I do and say. Thank You for the people who help me each day. Thank You for all You do for me. Amen.

Blind Bartimaeus

Bartimaeus was a blind man. Because he couldn't see, he wasn't able to find a job. Each day he sat next to the road and begged for money. He needed money so that he could buy something to eat and have a place to live. One day, Jesus and a crowd of people passed him on the road. He shouted out asking what was happening. When he found out it was Jesus, he called out even louder. Even though people told him to be quiet, he wouldn't stop. Jesus heard his cries and asked that the man be brought to Him. Jesus asked Bartimaeus what he wanted. Bartimaeus said that he wanted to see. Because he believed in Jesus, Bartimaeus could see again.

Thought Questions:

Close your eyes. What do you see? It's dark. You cannot see what's happening around you. Bartimaeus was blind and couldn't see anything. Close your eyes again and listen carefully. What do you hear? Maybe you hear a clock ticking or a bird singing. Even though you can't see, you can hear what is happening. Bartimaeus heard from the crowd that Jesus was approaching. How did Bartimaeus try to get Jesus' attention? When Jesus met Bartimaeus what miracle did He perform? Imagine how excited Bartimaeus must have been to see all the colors and people around him. Jesus had given him the gift of sight.

Prayer:

Dear Jesus, Thank You for the gift of sight. Thank You that I can hear the Bible stories and see the pictures. I praise You for the many blessing You have given me. Amen.

Zacchaeus

Zacchaeus knew Jesus was coming to the town of Jericho. He wanted to see Jesus. Zacchaeus had a problem. He was very short and couldn't see over the crowd. He knew the route Jesus was taking. There was a large sycamore tree on the side of the road. Zacchaeus quickly climbed the tree. As Jesus passed by, He looked up and spotted Zacchaeus. Jesus said to him, "Zacchaeus, come down immediately. I must stay at your house today." Zacchaeus scampered down the tree and took Jesus to his home. Not only had Zacchaeus seen Jesus, but he was going to have Jesus as a guest.

_____

Thought Questions:

Have you ever been to a parade or another event where you couldn't see? Did one of your parents lift you up so you could see? You had the same problem as Zacchaeus. Because Zacchaeus was an adult, he was not going to ask anyone to lift him up to see. What did Zacchaeus do to see Jesus? Because Zacchaeus was in the tree, it was easier for Jesus to see him too. What did Jesus ask Zacchaeus? Zacchaeus was very excited to take Jesus to his home.

Prayer:

Dear Jesus, even though I am small, I know You love me. Thank You for caring for all people. It doesn't matter if they are short, tall, sick, or healthy. Help me to be kind to all people. Amen.

Triumphal Entry

Jesus traveled to the capital city of Israel named Jerusalem. Jesus rode into the city on a donkey. In the past, a king of Israel would enter the city on a donkey. The crowds of people cheered as Jesus entered. They spread their coats on the ground in front of Him as He went by them. They waved palm branches as flags. The crowd yelled, "Blessed is the king who comes in the name of the Lord!" Luke 19:38 (NIV). Not everyone was happy to see the crowds cheering Jesus. Some didn't believe Jesus was God's Son. They wanted Him to stop preaching to the people. They also started to plan ways to hurt Jesus.

_____

Thought Questions:
Look at the picture of Jesus. What is He riding? Jesus rode a donkey that no one had ever ridden before. This was also how other kings of Israel entered Jerusalem. Do you see the crowds of people? What are they doing? As a sign of respect, the people put their coats on the ground. They also waved palm branches like we might wave a flag at a parade. We call the day that Jesus entered the city of Jerusalem "Palm Sunday." Some churches have children sing and wave palm branches on this special Sunday.

Prayer:
Dear Jesus, Thank You for being our King. Help us to praise You like the crowds of people in Jerusalem. Thank You for giving me a voice to sing Your praises. Amen.

The Last Supper

Jesus knew that there were leaders in Jerusalem who did not like Him. These people were trying to hurt Him. Jesus wanted His disciples to remember who He was and what He taught them. Jesus prepared a special meal for His disciples. This meal became known as the Last Supper. During the meal, Jesus broke bread and gave it to His disciples. Jesus told them that broken bread was to remind them of His body which was broken for their sins. Jesus went on to tell them that the drink He gave them was a reminder of the blood He would shed. The disciples did not know then that Jesus would die for their sins.

Thought Questions:

Churches hold a special service to remember Jesus' Last Supper with His disciples. The church service is called communion. Can you say the word communion? During the service, people eat pieces of bread. They remember that Jesus' body was broken for their sins. The people in church drink grape juice to remind them that Jesus' blood was shed for their sins. Even though the first Lord's Supper or Communion was a long time ago, people still remember what Jesus did for them.

Prayer:

Dear Lord, Bless my daily food and drink. Thank You for saving me from my sins. Help me to show each day that I love You. Amen.

Crucifixion

The leaders who disliked Jesus had Him arrested. They also planned for Jesus' death. Sadly, Jesus' disciples and mother watched as He was placed on a cross to die. Jesus knew that He needed to die so that the sins of all who loved Him could be forgiven. After suffering on the cross, Jesus called out, "It is finished!" John 19:30 (NIV). Jesus had completed His work to pay for the sins of His people. Jesus died for our sins. The disciples took His body down from the cross. They gently laid His body in a tomb. All of Jesus' friends went home. They were sad about the death of Jesus.

Thought Questions:
Look at the picture that goes with today's Bible story. It is a very sad scene. Do you see the man on the cross? That is Jesus. Why was Jesus put on a cross to die? Jesus died to forgive our sins. Do you see Jesus' friends? What did they do after He died? Jesus was placed in a tomb. Later, the disciples would go to the tomb to remember their friend, Jesus.

Prayer:
Dear Jesus, I am sorry when I sin and do bad things. Please forgive me. Thank You for dying on the cross for my sins. Amen.

Jesus' Resurrection

Three days after Jesus died, some women went to His tomb. When they arrived, they saw the stone was rolled away from the tomb. When they entered the tomb, there was no body. It was empty. Jesus was gone! Suddenly two angels appeared in front of them. The angels told them that Jesus was not dead. He was alive! Jesus had risen from the dead. The women ran to tell the disciples what they had seen and heard. At first the disciples did not believe the women. Two of the disciples, Peter and John, ran to the tomb to see if what the women said was true. They too saw the empty tomb. Just as He had told His disciples, Jesus had risen from the dead.

Thought Questions:

Easter is a special holiday for Christians. It is the day they praise God that Jesus rose from the dead. Look at the picture for today's lesson. When the women went to the tomb, what did they expect to see? They expected to see a tomb with a stone in front of it. What did they see instead? The angels told the women that Jesus had risen from the dead. What did the women do when they heard the news? They told the disciples. The news of Jesus' resurrection was too exciting to keep quiet. Christians today must also share the good news of Jesus' resurrection.

Prayer:

Dear Jesus, Thank You for dying for my sins. Thank You for rising from the dead. Help me to praise You as my Savior. Amen.

Ascension

After Jesus rose from the dead, He spent forty days preaching and teaching. His followers were able to see and hear their risen Savior. After forty days it was time for Jesus to return to His home in heaven. Jesus took His disciples to a place to talk to them. As He was talking, He was taken up to heaven. A cloud hid Jesus from their view. The disciples continued to look toward heaven. Suddenly two angels appeared to them. The angels told them that Jesus had been taken into heaven. One day He will return again.

Thought Questions:
After Jesus' resurrection, He continued to teach His disciples and followers. Do you remember how many days Jesus preached after His resurrection? He preached for forty days. After forty days where did Jesus go? He went back to His home in heaven. Jesus had finished His work on earth. He had preached to the people, died on the cross for their sins, and risen from the dead. Now in heaven Jesus continues to care for His people.

Prayer:
Dear Jesus, I praise You as my Savior. Thank You for being in heaven where You can hear my prayers. Amen.

The Disciples Preach

Before Jesus went back to heaven, He told the disciples they were to share the good news He had taught them. They were to go all over the world to tell people how Jesus came to earth to die for their sins. Not everyone wanted to hear the good news of Jesus. Sometimes the disciples were beaten or put in jail for what they said. This did not keep them from sharing the good news of Jesus. Today Christians still tell others the story of Jesus. Some of these people are missionaries. They often live far from home so they can tell others about Jesus. You too can share the story of Jesus with your family, friends, and other people you meet.

Thought Questions:

Before Jesus returned to heaven, He gave His disciples an important job. Do you remember the job He gave them? The disciples were to spread the good news of Jesus. Were people always excited to hear what the disciples preached? What bad things happened to them? Even though not everyone was excited to hear the disciples' words, many people were. They became followers of Christ. Some of the people who spread the good news of Jesus today are called missionaries. Many churches pray for specific missionaries. See if you can find a picture of one of the missionaries from your church or another church. Take time to pray each day for this missionary.

Prayer:

Dear Jesus, Thank You for sending Your disciples to share Your good news. Bless me as I share with others the stories from the Bible. Help all the missionaries that spread Your good news. Amen.

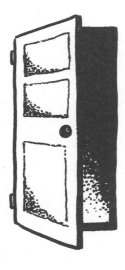

642

PLACES TO DRAW

CHRONICLE BOOKS

SAN FRANCISCO

Library of Congress Cataloging-in-Publication Data available.

ISBN: 978-1-4521-2493-3

Manufactured in China.

Design by Eloise Leigh

10 9 8 7 6 5 4 3 2 1

Chronicle Books LLC
680 Second Street
San Francisco, CA 94107

www.chroniclebooks.com

under your bed

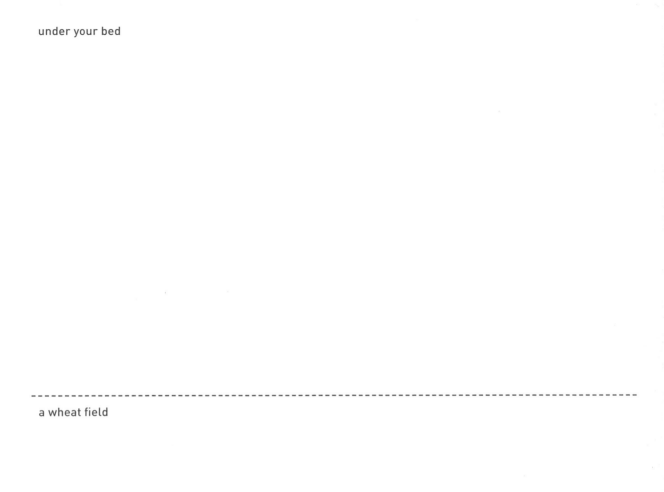

a wheat field

a haberdashery

a public swimming pool

a mossy grove deep in the woods

a bird nest

a paperboy training academy

a multilevel tree house

a haunted castle

an African savannah

a marathon finish line

a mouse hole

a tiny pyramid

an oil refinery

the land of faerie

the London Underground

---

a Little League concession stand

a runway at JFK airport

----

a construction site

----

an Irish pub

a city in the clouds

---

a nuclear power plant

---

the Grand Mosque in Mecca

a tollbooth

a high school hallway

a Bollywood movie set

a locker room

a paper mill

a milk bar

the Taj Mahal

a starting point

a secret passageway

a lumberyard

---

a Wisconsin dairy farm

---

a train yard

a raised drawbridge

a linen closet

the basket of a hot-air balloon

an emergency room waiting area

a Prohibition-era speakeasy

a chicken coop

a darkroom

a beach souvenir shop

Machu Picchu

the White House

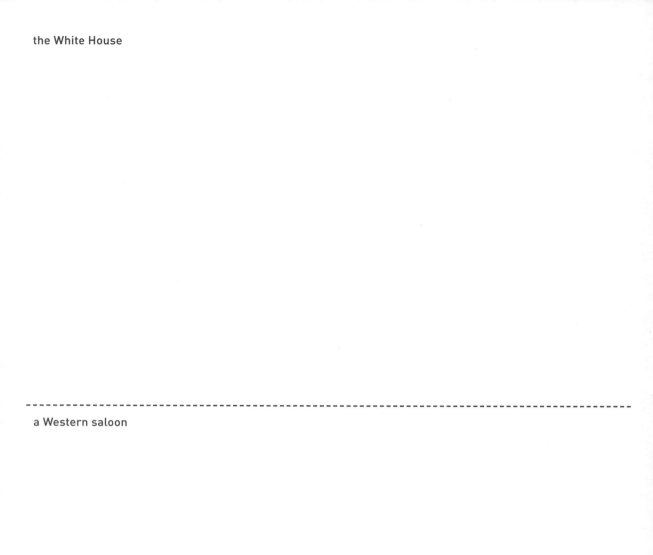

a Western saloon

the Catskills in fall   a winding road a clear-cut mountainside

----

an orchestra pit

Land's End, England | the Turkish embassy

Santa's workshop | a helicopter landing pad

inside a confessional

under a rock

under the boardwalk

a public restroom

a lost city

a rooftop garden

---

a private beach

backstage at an elementary school play

----

a Yangtze River floodplain

----

a coal mine

your childhood home

Paris in the springtime

the top of the world

where the sidewalk ends

a bargain grocery store

a luxury car showroom

a Maine crab shack

a shooting range

a shady lane

the Sicilian coast

Candy Land

up on a high wire

----

a busy lunch counter

----

base camp on Mount Everest

an Italian monastery

a forest foot path

on a high dive

a roadside produce stand

a mall food court

the English Channel during a storm

an oasis

the first class cabin

an '80s video arcade

an evening news studio

a flooded neighborhood

a pond in a city park

- -

a long, hot dirt road

- -

a mini-mart

a barbershop

a movie projector booth

Red Square

a runaway truck ramp

Monet's flower garden

the backseat

the middle of nowhere

a lonely crossroads

between a rock and a hard place

a community garden

a wax museum

----
a rose garden

Valhalla

an agave cactus farm

a rain forest

a potter's studio

Japantown

a wedding dress stockroom

the Thames River under fog

over the moon

Except there's no
gravity in space.
only towards and
away from

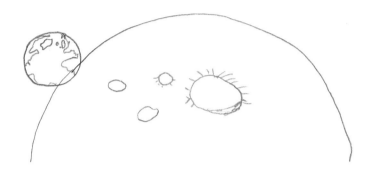

- -

an antebellum theater

a lion's den

----

a horse corral

a hospital nursery

the Black Hills

a postage stamp museum

the Roman Colosseum

the lair of an evil genius

the Khyber Pass

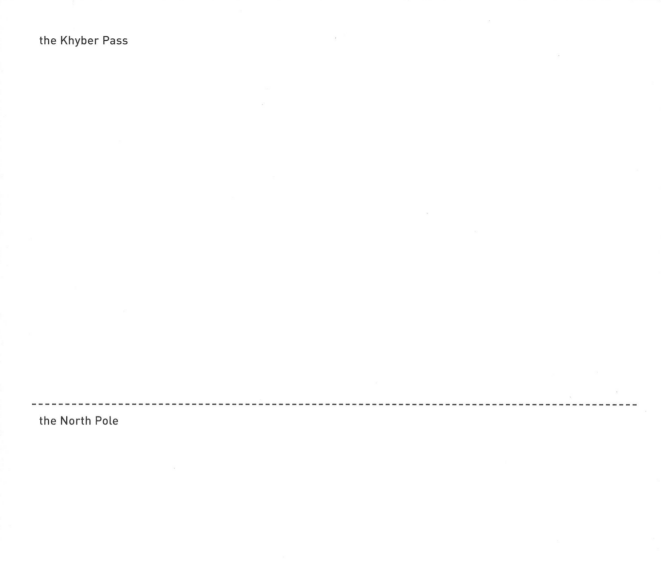

the North Pole

inside Big Ben

a wine cellar

a brewery

----

a vacant lot

----

a flower conservatory

a sunshine factory

Main Street, America

a tattoo parlor

a wind farm

the middle of the Atlantic Ocean

an Elks lodge

a used-car dealership

a driving school obstacle course

inside an elevator

a fishing hole

a cat lady's living room

---

a New York subway platform

---

the Strait of Gibraltar

a roadhouse

---

a kibbutz

---

a loading dock

Central Park in the middle of summer

a velodrome

a logging camp

a horse stable

a frontier cabin

a thrift store

---

an inner-city playground

a multilevel parking structure

a bat cave

a pumpkin patch

a polo field

the Moulin Rouge

a squirrel hole

the Forbidden City

the Crystal Palace

a college lecture hall

---

under the kitchen table

terraced rice fields

a cheese cave

a dive bar

an office mailroom

a folk art museum

---

the Treasury at Petra

---

a barrel maker's yard

a bike shop

a sumo ring

---

boot camp

a tanning salon

a shipwreck on the ocean floor

a Christmas tree farm

a high-altitude sheep pasture

an underground city

----

a yard sale

a cruise ship boiler room

atop a microscopic speck

Woodstock, New York, August 1969 | a cozy booth in an Indian restaurant

a dojo | an empty apartment

an herb garden

---

a mangrove swamp

---

a pecan grove

a mannequin storeroom

- -

a fireworks superstore

the restaurant at Mount Rushmore

the French Quarter

Checkpoint Charlie

Chichen Itza

a casino floor

the dock of the bay

on top of Mount Olympus

a salt marsh

an inlet

a Mongolian grassland

a boathouse beside a lake

an Austrian ski lodge

a Broadway theater

the surface of the moon

an airport boarding gate

a field of sunflowers

a country club

---

a circle of flags

Versailles

a rocky cliff

King Solomon's mines

a vampire's bedroom

sleep-away camp | a Spanish bullring

the O.K. Corral | a Roach Motel

the Golden Gate Bridge at sunset

Sagrada Família

a cider house at harvest time

a Georgia peach orchard

a dog park

a masquerade ball

the center of the universe

a vineyard

----

the snake house at the zoo

Coney Island

a pigsty

a bagel place

downtown Chicago on St. Patty's Day

a chocolate factory

a late-night diner

an interstate median

a valley of windmills in Holland

the white cliffs of Dover

a junkyard

a prehistoric settlement

Timbuktu

a power plant

----

a county fair

the Indianapolis 500

a metalsmith's workshop

an arctic research station

a Spanish mission

Treasure Island

---

a stock car racetrack

---

the banks of the Mississippi River

the Australian outback

Mount Vesuvius

the back of your closet

a Hobbit hole

a dry cleaner

Tierra del Fuego

a '70s disco

the Valley of the Dolls

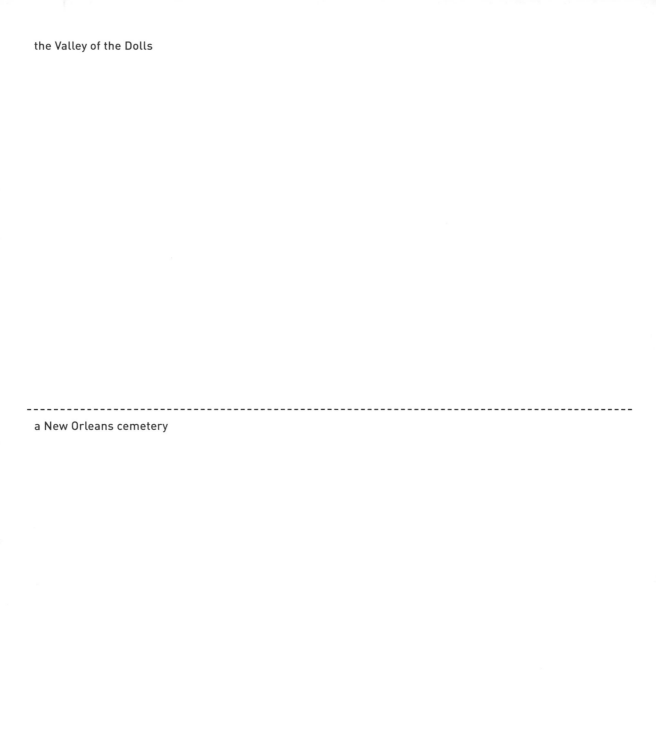

----

a New Orleans cemetery

cruising altitude at thirty thousand feet

an archeological dig

a Norse banquet hall | a Venetian canal

a glacial lake

a Scottish golf course

Easter Island

a cubbyhole

Neverland

the center of a tornado

the point of no return

a strip mall in Texas

a roller-skating rink

a yoga retreat

---

the top shelf of your pantry

a royal wedding

a Buddhist temple

a nursing home hallway

Hogwarts Castle

Rockefeller Center at Christmas

a covered bridge in New Hampshire

----

a foggy Irish coast

----

a dry creek

the factory floor of a steel mill

a Japanese tea pavilion

----

the Acropolis full of tourists

the Petronas Towers

Victoria Falls

Graceland

Mount Fuji wrapped in mist

the *Mona Lisa*'s private room at the Louvre

a Southern catfish fry

Times Square on New Year's Eve

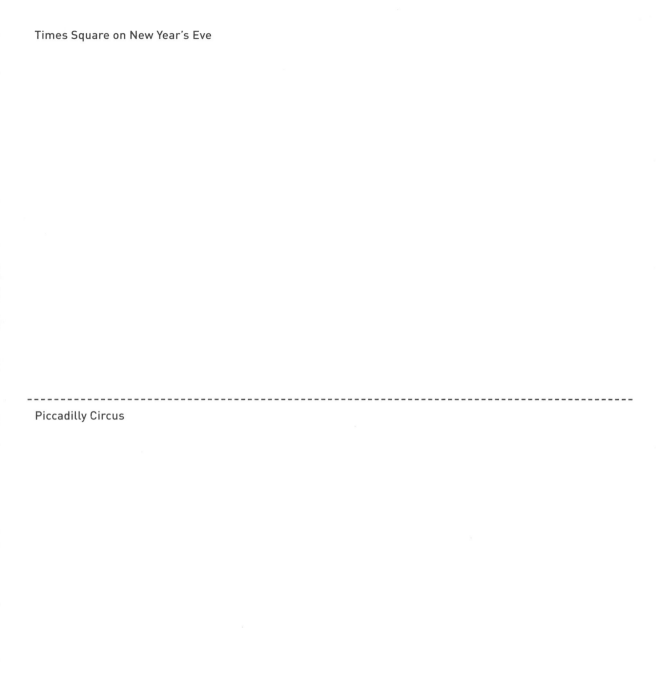

Piccadilly Circus

Loch Ness

the Wailing Wall

the Eiffel Tower in winter  a prison guard-tower at night

a rodeo

---

a Dutch tulip farm

---

a snowed-in village

a bowling alley

the trading floor of the New York Stock Exchange

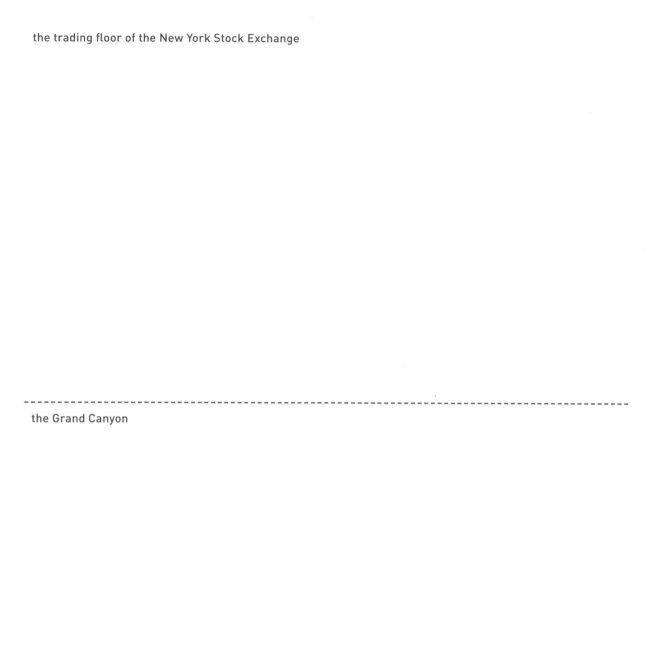

the Grand Canyon

the Gateway Arch

Stonehenge when it was first built

Mont St. Michel

a Quaker meetinghouse

Capitol Hill during a protest

a coin-op car wash

the Cape of Good Hope

a sandbar

a gravel pit

a dodgy pool room

Angkor Wat

a Bavarian castle

the Space Needle

dunes in the Sahara desert

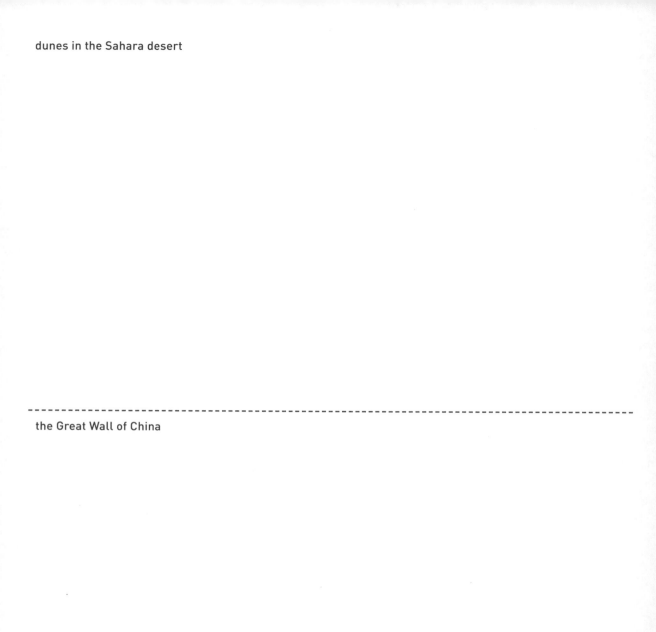

the Great Wall of China

Little Bighorn

----

the Kentucky Derby

Fallingwater, Pennsylvania

----

a cranberry bog

----

the Great Smoky Mountains

a medieval dungeon

an office break room

Uluru (Ayers Rock)

deep left in a baseball field

the Hollywood Hills

----

a drive-in movie

Thomas Edison's laboratory

a Norwegian fjord

the cave where the Dead Sea Scrolls were found

Old Faithful

a pitcher's mound

the Valley of the Kings

----

a truck stop

----

a hammock on a beach in Key West

the city of the future

a batting cage

Colonial Williamsburg

a Jewish deli

a riverbank

an Olympic gymnasium

a meteor crater

----

an outdoor gospel revival

the US/Canadian border

----

a trailer park at dusk

the St. Lawrence Seaway flowing into the Atlantic

---

the tunnel of love

Grand Central Terminal at rush hour

the Grand Bazaar

a freshman dorm room

a little house on the prairie

the Land of Ten Thousand Lakes

Gettysburg

an airport coffee kiosk

a greenhouse filled with rare orchids

Williamsburg, Brooklyn

a '60s beach party

---

a coatroom at the opera

a used-book store

the Washington Monument

the Cristo Redentor statue overlooking Rio de Janeir

Lake Superior

----

the Everglades

----

a college football tailgating party

a surgical theater

the Palace of Knossos

a petrified forest

----

a recycling center

a VIP box at the World Series

221b Baker Street

a Tuscan villa

a locals-only surf spot

the banks of the Amazon River

a science fair

a red-light district

----

opening day at Wrigley Field

the Egyptian Wing at the Met

St. Peter's Basilica

Downton Abbey

a storm cellar

the cockpit of a fighter plane

the Tower of Babel

a deep ocean trench

a country church

a river levee

a fishing village in Okinawa

a cantina in the Yucatan

a throne room

a hiding place

a 1920s swing club

Portobello Road

an abandoned theme park

a go-cart race

----

a Florida alligator farm

----

the launch site at Cape Canaveral

a sculpture park

Sleepy Hollow

----
an international youth hostel

a Pacific Northwest fish market

a suburban cul-de-sac

a grassy knoll

a toolshed

an overgrown backyard

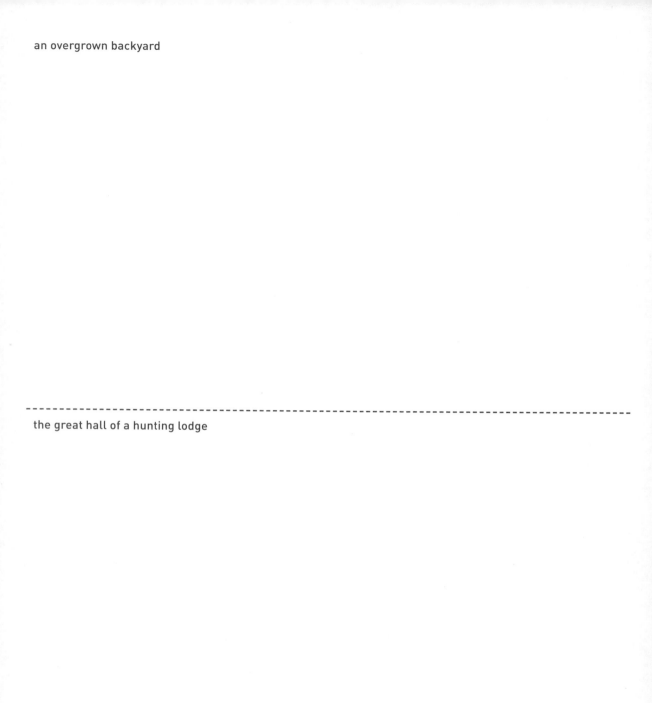

the great hall of a hunting lodge

a Swiss chalet

Tiananmen Square

a fault line

one mile of an oil pipeline

Death Valley

an overlook on a coastal highway

---

an island landing strip

---

inside the CERN particle accelerator

inside a voting booth

Redwood National Park

a planetarium during a Pink Floyd laser show

hog heaven

among friends

a space observatory

- -

a captain's quarters

a doughnut shop

a bank vault

the Rock and Roll Hall of Fame

a town square

a one-room schoolhouse

a bocce ball court

the Atlantic City boardwalk

the Berlin Wall before it fell

a modern dance studio

an inaugural ball

----

a tiki bar

----

the catacombs under Paris

Luxembourg

a cardboard box fort

the crow's nest of a pirate ship

mission control at NASA

a hedge maze

Ali Baba's cave

the Arc de Triomphe

a walk-in cooler

a koi pond

a marble quarry

the Spanish Steps

a pizzeria in Naples

the Alamo

the Las Vegas Strip

a barrel over Niagara Falls

an airplane bathroom

the Roman Forum

----

a German biergarten

Buckingham Palace

the Parthenon

a town hall meeting

a safari tent

the Oval Office

an antiques auction

----

a studio apartment

Sesame Street

Atlantis

Camelot

the poppy field in front of the Emerald City

a long way from home

a dugout house

the Old Curiosity Shop

the Sistine Chapel

a patch of sunlight

a life-sized gingerbread house

the *New York Times* newsroom

----

an aquarium

the House of the Rising Sun

---

a garage specializing in luxury cars

the Black Forest

a powder room

----

a high school science lab

----

a department store Santaland

the Panama Canal

a zeppelin hangar

a deep sea oil rig

a tiger pit

the interior of the sun

a monster truck rally

- -

the Death Star

the Sydney Opera House

a dentist's office

Boston Common

a firehouse bunkroom

a soup kitchen

a train sleeper car

the Hanging Gardens of Babylon

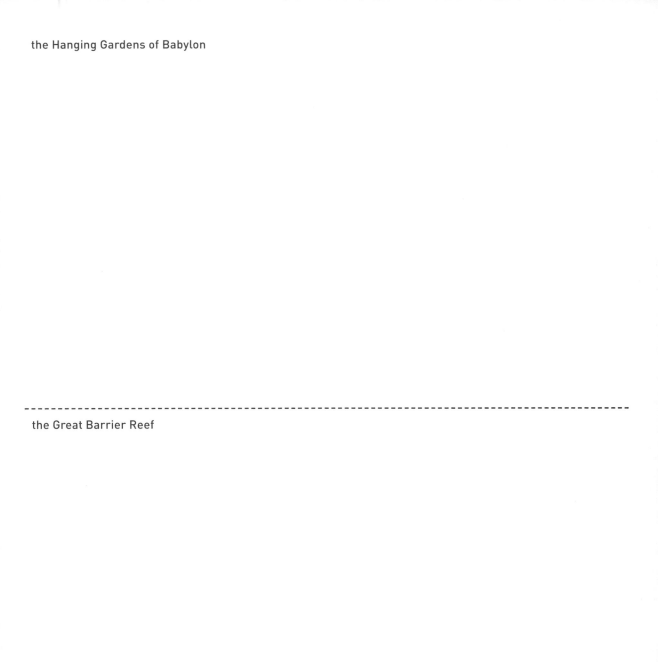

----

the Great Barrier Reef

the Hoover Dam

- -

the Guggenheim

- -

an English moor

a swimming hole

an Old West jail

a pick-your-own blueberry farm

the Champs-Élysées at sunset

an ant farm

an icehouse

Earth

the Galapagos Islands

approaching Monaco from the sea

paddling into class-four rapids

Fort Knox

Harvard Square

a bird sanctuary

a hall of mirrors

a lighthouse on a foggy night

the Grand Ole Opry

----

a Himalayan tea plantation

----

a Laundromat

a cluttered attic

a punk band's practice space

----

inside a yurt

the cereal aisle

Palm Springs

an ice crevasse

Kensington Gardens

the New Jersey Turnpike

an Oxford University library

the Super Bowl

the Plaza Hotel

El Dorado

Strawberry Fields

the rings of Saturn

the International Space Station

Joshua Tree

- -
Tijuana

a bingo hall

Bourbon Street

----

a Revolutionary War outpost

your grandmother's kitchen

the Jelly Belly factory

a wraparound front porch

a Brussels sprout field

a Russian Orthodox cathedral

Rock 'n' Roll High School   a landfill

a quilt show

----

a dude ranch

a bottling plant

a Barbie Dream House

a wormhole

a butterfly habitat

Area 51

a car assembly line

an aircraft carrier

the Sri Lankan jungle during monsoon season

----

the tennis courts at Wimbledon

a ramen restaurant

the Temple of Doom

where the action is

Alcatraz Island

---

a Greenwich Village coffee house

Lincoln's log cabin

a tractor pull

a pancake house

a house of cards

the River Styx

a shoe house

a fish hatchery

a golf course sand trap

a shotgun house

Utopia

a million-dollar doghouse

Venice Beach

a ravine

a promenade

the dinosaur room at the Museum of Natural History

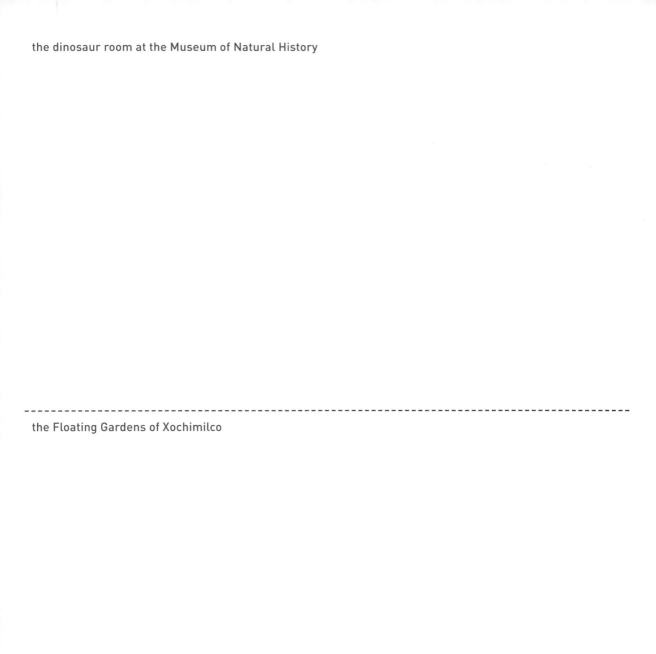

----

the Floating Gardens of Xochimilco

the land before time

a smokehouse

----

the Rose Parade

----

the Scottish Highlands

a china shop

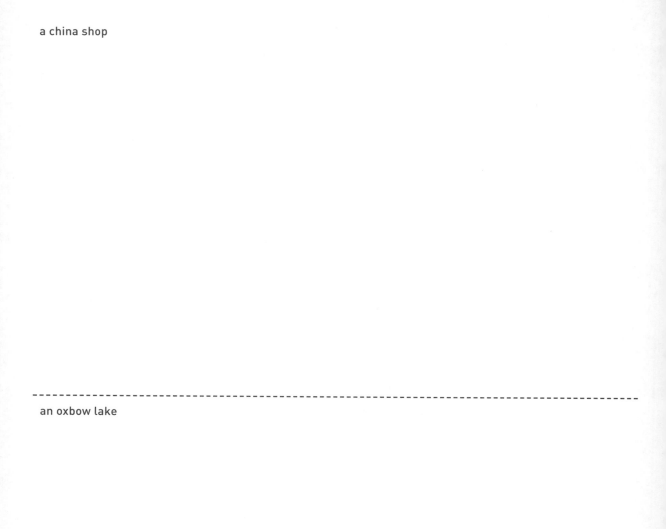

an oxbow lake

a bus stop

Dollywood

in the pines

Cannery Row

---

a hardware store

the bell tower of an English village

a karaoke box

out of this world

the eye of the storm

an Elvis-themed birthday party

a quiet study

in a New York cab

snow-capped mountains

a WWF Slamfest

----

a mirage

the Bering Strait, seventeen thousand years ago

a weather station in Alaska

the bulk section of a health food store

a natural bridge

a Western ghost town

the Statue of Liberty

a grotto at high tide

a Cherokee village

LOVE Park, Philadelphia

----

an outdoor ice hockey rink

the Canadian Potato Museum

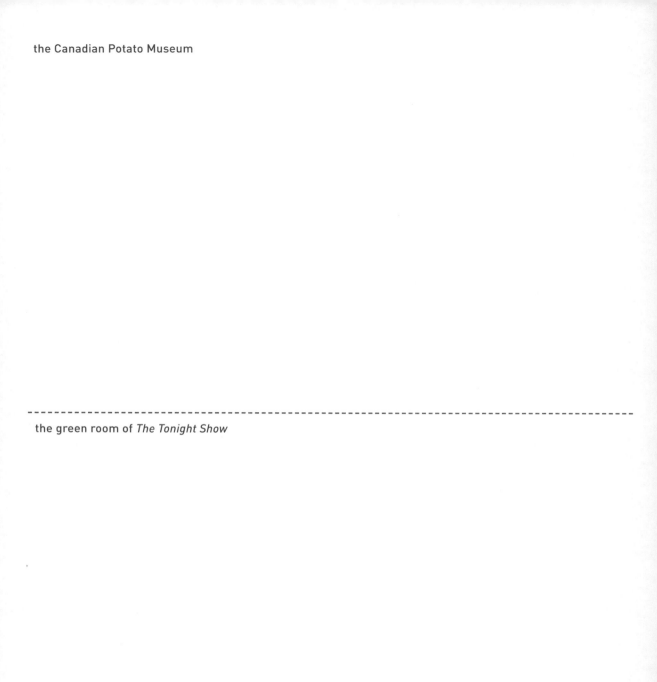

the green room of *The Tonight Show*

a portrait studio

the Corn Palace

the wrong side of the tracks

the witness stand

Devils Tower

a farmers' bank

a bamboo forest

your favorite place

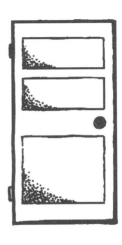